W9-ARU-662

dedicated to:

....

....

....

celebrating
friends

share, remember, cherish

JIM McCANN, FOUNDER

**Andrews McMeel
Publishing, LLC**

Kansas City • Sydney • London

Andrews McMeel Publishing, LLC
an Andrews McMeel Universal company
1130 Walnut Street, Kansas City, Missouri 64106

www.andrewsmcmeel.com

11 12 13 14 15 SMA 10 9 8 7 6 5 4 3 2 1

ISBN: 978-1-4494-0824-4

Library of Congress Control Number: 2011926177

ATTENTION: SCHOOLS AND BUSINESSES

Andrews McMeel books are available at quantity discounts with bulk purchase for
educational, business, or sales promotional use. For information, e-mail the Andrews
McMeel Publishing Special Sales Department: specialsales@amuniversal.com.

Project Manager and Editor: Heidi Tyline King

Designed by Alexis Siroc

Produced by SMALLWOOD & STEWART, INC., NEW YORK CITY

Illustration credit information on page 70.

INTRODUCTION

WHEN I LOOK BACK at the important events in my life, both big and small, I realize that I have shared just about every one of them with a friend. There are my childhood friends, the guys from my old neighborhood who still know me as "Jimmy from Richmond Hill." We may not see each other on a regular basis, but when we do play catch-up, the years melt away and we settle into a familiarity and intimacy as only old friends can.

I also have business friends, people I speak with or see on a routine basis who challenge and support me professionally. Just recently, one of these friends retired, only to return to work a few months later. "Why come back?" I asked. He explained, "I realized that I had fewer friends when I didn't work because I really had no reason to speak with them." I understood, because the relationships I have through work are among the primary reasons I enjoy what I do so much.

There are unlikely friendships—some of my "friends" on Facebook and the people I meet on airplanes or at parties, such as the young man and woman that captivated my wife, Mary Lou, and I during a recent trip to Barcelona. We were presenters at the same conference, and an impromptu dinner date led to one of those glorious, magical nights that don't come along very often. The food was great, the waiters serenaded our table, and Mary Lou and I reveled in the hours of great conversation we had with these two young kids. That night was the beginning of new friend- ships that we've continued after returning home.

And then there is a friend who is closer than a brother—or in my case, a close friend who just happens to be my brother. Chris is 10 years younger than I, and we've worked together for 30 years. Let's just say that the guy knows me like no one else. He gets my jokes. He laughs along with me at my stupid mistakes. He keeps me grounded—and he loves me, no matter what.

Because it takes all kinds of friends to get us through the battlefield of life, we at 1-800-FLOWERS.com thought it appropriate that a book on friendship be part of our *Celebrating . . .* series. It may be a cliché, but friends really do make the world go round. I find that my overall well-being and happiness lie in direct correlation with how connected I feel to my "friend universe." Hearing from a friend out of the blue always lifts my spirits and adds a little bit of specialness to an otherwise ordinary day. I hope this book does the same for you.

So go ahead—raise your glass in a toast. Write that note you've been meaning to send. Call and check in on the friend—old or new—who has been on your mind. Underline a favorite story in this book and drop it in the mail to a friend—just because. That's what *Celebrating Friends* is all about: sharing, remembering, and cherishing the people and relationships that matter most.

ONE

fun friends

as a child, I would always tell my best friend at summer camp: "A friend is someone who knows the song in your heart and can sing it back to you when you have forgotten the words." —JULIE K.

Animals are such
agreeable friends—
they ask no questions,
they pass no criticisms.

—GEORGE ELIOT

My best friend brought me a vitamin
every day in first grade. Now, thirty years later,
she's still the best vitamin around!

—CANDY G.

All the world old is strange
save thee and me, and even
thou art a little strange.

—ROBERT OWEN

The Language of Friendship

Arabic ... sahib

Bulgarian ... priiatel

Catalan ... amic

Chinese ... peng you

Czech ... pratele

Danish ... ven

English ... friend

Estonian ... soprus

French ... ami(e)

German ... freund

Hawaiian ... hoa aloha

Hebrew ... yedeed(a)

Hungarian ... barat

Indonesian ... handai

Italian ... amico(a)

Japanese ... ami

Latin ... amicus

Russian ... drug

Spanish ... amigo(a)

Swedish ... van

Yiddish ... fraynd

The holy passion of friendship is of so sweet and steady and loyal and enduring a nature that it will last through a whole lifetime, if not asked to lend money.

—MARK TWAIN

No people feel closer or more friendly than those who are on the same diet. —ANONYMOUS

Friend
to Friend:
"It's no coincidence
we'd end up here at
the same time . . .
with a popcorn large
enough for sharing!"

—JESSE B.

Root beer and cornbread—that's the first snack I ever had at my best friend's house. We were in fifth grade and lived in the same neighborhood, went to the same elementary school. I didn't even like root beer, but drank it anyway to be polite. The cornbread was excellent, though. At age 27, we're still best friends, despite the root beer, which I still don't like. —SUSAN

In honor of Friendship Day,
Winnie the Pooh was named as the
world's Ambassador of Friendship
at the United Nations in 1997.

A workplace without friends is an enemy.

—*THE WASHINGTON POST*

Everyone can stand to make a few new friends. Try these techniques the next time you find yourself in a situation surrounded by new people:

+ *Focus on someone else.* Listen attentively and affirm him by repeating something he said in the conversation.

+ *Watch body language.* You can learn a lot about a person through observation.

+ *Keep your negative thoughts to yourself.* No one likes a party pooper, especially if you have just met.

+ *Find a common activity* that you can do together to take your "new" friendship a step further.

+ *Be friendly and approachable.* Don't forget that other people are often just as scared—or more so— of being rejected as you are.

*Good friends are the sprinkle
to my sundae.*

—MARIA D.

What kind of friend are you?

A study by Microsoft in the United Kingdom categorizes people into four types of friends:

- **Cultivators** regard friendship with great value. These people **nurture friendships** and **initiate interaction**.

- **Pruners** make friends and then drop them just as fast. They like **to be seen** in the "in crowd."

- **Harvesters** have an **inner circle of friends**, even if they don't speak on a routine basis.

- **Gatherers make friends easily** but do little to make the effort to keep in touch.

A true friend
knows your real
weight and age.

—ANONYMOUS

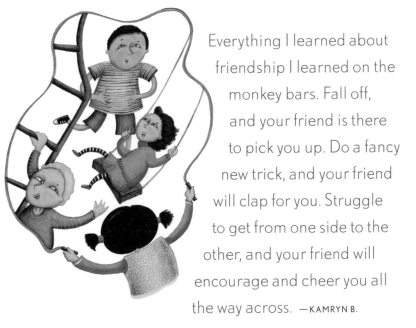

Everything I learned about friendship I learned on the monkey bars. Fall off, and your friend is there to pick you up. Do a fancy new trick, and your friend will clap for you. Struggle to get from one side to the other, and your friend will encourage and cheer you all the way across. —KAMRYN B.

My best friend is . . .

. . . the icing on my birthday cake. —ASHTON S.

. . . the peanut butter to my jelly. —KAMARI Y.

. . . the rainbow in my clouds. —MONIQUE A.

. . . the bee on my flower. —ROMAN L.

. . . the bottle cap on my bottle. —JAMAL C.

Friendship is like an endless supply of chocolate.

—GAVINO Z.

through thick and thin

On the road
between the homes of friends,
grass does not grow.

—NORWEGIAN PROVERB

My mother is my best friend. She's the one who taught me that things don't always happen for the best; it's that we must make the best of the things that happen.

—RUTH P.

Scientists have found that
men and women view friendship
differently. For women, friendship
is a face-to-face relationship;
for men, it's side-by-side.

even as a child, *I have always loved flowers. I was constantly rearranging my mother's silk flower arrangements, and my cousin Darlene would always cheer me on. When I was 16, she pointed out my talent and gave me the idea that perhaps I was good enough to one day become a florist. Well here I am, 24 years later, a floral designer who continues to be inspired and challenged in both my professional and personal lives by none other than dear Darlene.* —ADAM L.

When I miss my bus, my mom is always there to pick me up.

—BRIAN G.

Anybody can make do when things are flush. Loyalty is the thing that will help you through the bad times. —JIM MCCANN

What do you say when your husband says, "You need to move out"? In my case, it was music to my ears! You see, I had a home business that had outgrown our home, and rather than being able to recognize my own success, it took my husband stepping in to tell me that I was good enough—and capable—to officially open a storefront. He has been my husband all these years, but even more, he has been my one true, constant friend. —ELIZABETH O.

The kind of friend that I will be is the kind **who cares when you are up or down**.

I'll **make you laugh** when times are tough, and help you see the light at the end of the tunnel when things seem hopelessly dark.

I will **share your joys**, and cheer you on through your aspirations.

I will be the **friend who is honest** enough to tell you that your new dress doesn't do you justice—even as I am reminding you that I am not the fashion editor at the local paper.

I will **encourage you** to reach your goals, whether it is to shed 10 pounds or run a marathon.

I will **step in and help** when life schedules you to be in 15 places at the same time.

I will **share with you the lessons learned** when I have failed, so that you will succeed in your own way.

I will **be your biggest fan**, because the world has enough critics.

I will **be there at every milestone**, and we will cherish it with grace.

I will **hold your hand** when you are facing a health crisis, and **give you my shoulder** when a loved one's life journey comes to an end.

I will be this kind of friend to you, **because you are this kind of friend to me**. —JENNY G.

*Friends know how to be happy for you
even when they are sad for themselves.*

—NATASHA P.

*A friend may well be reckoned
the masterpiece of nature.*

—RALPH WALDO EMERSON

A dear friend of mine is one of the sweetest girls you will ever meet—except when she is around me. I was so puzzled by this that one time I asked her, "Why do you only get mad at me?"

"That's because you're a real friend," she said.

I was confused. "What do you mean?" I asked.

"Unfortunately, you sometimes get to see the real me—and you still forgive me and put up with me," she explained.

That's when I realized what being a true friend is all about—accepting each other's good and bad personality traits—and loving each other anyway. —CHELSEA R.

ven though I am in middle school, one of my best friends is my older cousin, Annie. I've always looked up to Annie and she has always been great about sharing her advice on school, running track, and even boys. But I never realized how important she was to me until she left for college this past fall. I knew I could text her every day, but I was worried that we might not stay as close.

Amazingly, being apart has deepened our friendship and made us closer in a way that I never would have expected to be so powerful—through letters, handwritten on paper and mailed in envelopes with stamps. I have discovered that the whole process of writing a letter has made us both open up more and share our feelings. Texting may be a great way to talk to my friends in town quickly, but only letters from my cousin far away in college can make me laugh or cry—or both at the same time! —EMILY M.

You know you're a good friend when sacrifice comes as easy as smiling.

—JESSE B.

Friendship is what makes an alligator get along with a crocodile.

—JUSTIN G.

 he nicest thing my best friend ever did for me is the most recent. I was in New York, and I had to see my ex. It was very difficult for me, so she came with me. She didn't say much—she let my ex and me chat briefly, but once we moved on, my best friend looked at me and said, "You know, he was much more of a catch when he was with you. You made him more of a catch than he ever was or ever will be." She meant it, too. —KATHLEEN

"Baby, you can do it." No matter what I have tried to tackle in my life, my husband has always been there to cheer me on. When I decided to go back to college after 20 years, he insisted that nothing come between me and my degree—even when he was diagnosed with lung cancer. We spent many long nights together, me studying at his bedside in the hospital while he struggled to stay alive. Always, he would put aside his own physical and emotional pains to encourage me. He is in remission now, and I have my degree—and both can be credited to his perseverance and inspiring spirit. —TYANNA M.

Love is blind.
Friendship closes its eyes.

—PROVERB

Friendship: A Few Statistics

- Most people make *lifelong friendships* between the ages of 15 and 25.

- Six out of 10 people *value friendship* more than money, successful careers, and even family.

- Women who *visit with friends* regularly experience a 72 percent remission in depression—about the same success rate as antidepressants.

- Sixty-nine percent of women surveyed in a *Ladies Home Journal* poll said they have *enough friends* in their lives; 25 percent don't and wish they did. More than half consider their husband to be *their best friend.*

THREE

the joy of friends

WHEN I WAS A BOY, my father, uncles, and their friends would gather around my grandmother's table each evening after work. Everyone would have a Scotch and get mellow, and the stories would start flowing. I was as happy as a fly on the wall to sit back and listen to all this grown-up talk. There was no plan, no goal for these gatherings—just camaraderie and, most importantly, bonding. —JIM MCCANN

Friends are the people with whom you have the most memories—and the ones you couldn't imagine making those memories without. —NATASHA P.

According to researchers, overall closeness, contact, and supportiveness predict whether a good friendship is maintained. But only a single factor—social-identity support—predicts whether a friend is ultimately elevated to the position of "best friend." It seems that we become best friends with people who boost our self-esteem by affirming our identities as part of a certain group, such as mothers or teammates.

Two may talk together under the same roof for many years, yet never really meet; and two others at first speech are old friends. —MARY CATHERWOOD

. . . that person who can connect one~on~one with you~that's where the magic happens.

—JIM MCCANN

I felt it shelter to speak to you.

—EMILY DICKINSON

One morning, my friend and I were both late to school. Flustered, we came up with a grand idea. If we went to class late, we would have to go to detention. But, if we just skipped first period altogether, we wouldn't be marked tardy. Who could argue with that kind of logic? So we walked around, talking and giggling, until second period. But then, it hit us that if we were already marked as absent, we might as well take the whole day off.

So . . . for the next six weeks, neither of us attended a full day of high school. Surprisingly, our parents were never notified—that is, until "Pat," another student, turned me in to Vice Principal Roberts.

What happened after that set the tone for a friendship that has lasted thirty years. The next day, my friend marched into the office and turned herself in so I wouldn't have to suffer my punishment alone. I knew that any friend who would voluntarily walk through the valley of Old Man Roberts with me was a friend indeed. And she remains so to this day—through births and deaths and the comings and goings of good fortune, we are still best friends. —LINDA

The ingredients for friendship are:
3 tablespoons of unconditional love,
2 pounds of genuine companionship, and
1 scoop of uncontrollable laughter . . .
which makes a lifetime of great memories!

—TOBIAS T.

*A true friend will teach you how to
make coffee instead of getting you coffee.*

—YANIQUE W.

Friendship is a popular relationship to celebrate. Every day is a good day to honor friends, but to make it "official," mark your calendar for:

National Friendship **Day**

>>> first Sunday in August

Women's Friendship **Day**

>>> third Sunday in August

International Friendship **Month**

>>> February

International Old Friends, New Friends **Week**

>>> third week in May

A friend is someone you can speak to today, tomorrow and in one year, and pick right up where you left off.

—LISA H.

A meaningful friendship can never be measured by monetary means. —ANONYMOUS

A true friend will bring a smile
to your face even on the darkest of days.

—ANONYMOUS

Need a few reasons for nurturing your friendships?

- *Researchers have found that people with no friends increase their risk of death over a six-month period.*

- *People with the most friends over a nine-year period cut their risk of death by more than 60 percent.*

- *The more friends women have, the less likely they are to develop physical impairments as they age, and the more likely they are to lead joyful lives.*

- *Women who lose a spouse are more likely to survive the experience without any new physical impairments or loss of vitality when they have a close friend.*

A true friend keeps quiet when you lie about your age and your weight . . . unless you're lying to yourself.

—JOYA N.

I don't like to commit myself about heaven and hell—you see, I have friends in both places. —MARK TWAIN

friends
to the end

i was Day-Glo and bell-bottoms. Lisa was argyle and khakis. I was always in the show. Lisa was happy to be in the stage crew. In eighth grade, I was obsessed with *Miss Saigon*, while Lisa never missed an episode of *Days of Our Lives*.

As adults, Lisa has kids; I don't. She lives in a house in the suburbs. I am a city girl thriving on my apartment lifestyle. I still love being in the spotlight. She is happy in the background. She doesn't work. I work for myself. She drives everywhere, and I haven't been behind the wheel of a car for years.

Looking over our 20 years of friendship, I can think of only one thing we have ever had in common—our mutual love for each other. I love our differences, and though our friendship might seem odd to others, it makes sense to us. She's the sister I never had. But she's also more than a sister. She's my best friend.

—MICHELLE W.

Acquaintances are easy to come by,

Family we cannot choose,

But friends are the ones we fight for

And strive never to lose.

—NATASHA P.

We call that person who has lost his father, an orphan; and a widower, that man who has lost his wife. But that man who has known the immense unhappiness of losing a friend, by what name do we call him? Here every language is silent and holds its peace in impotence. —JOSEPH ROUX

Life without a friend is death without a witness.

—SPANISH PROVERB

Growing up, my Aunt Jeanie was my rock.
She taught me to be strong and independent. When I
struggled to keep afloat and needed a friend to confide
in, she told me to keep going no matter what life tosses at
you. To this day, I still live by her words of wisdom, and I
smile every time I see, think, or hear from her. —JEAN B.

What I would give for one more day, one more minute with my mother. Even though she died 20 years ago, I think of how strong, unafraid, and happy she was. She spent her last few days making sure we all knew she was going to be okay—and that we would be okay, too. She was, is, and always will be the inspiration in my life, and my best friend. —INA W.

One loyal friend is worth ten thousand relatives.

—EURIPIDES

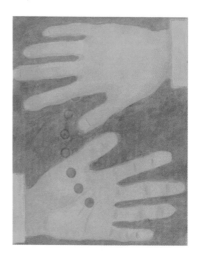

The Language of Friendship for Texters

143 .... I Love You

1432 .... I Love You, Too

2G2B4G .... Too Good to Be Forgotten

AF .... As a Friend; Always and Forever

BFF .... Best Friends Forever

BFFN .... Best Friends for Now

BFFTTE .... Best Friends Forever 'Til the End

GBH .... Great Big Hug

121 .... One-to-One

WUWH .... Wish You Were Here

YTB .... You're the Best

GYB .... Got Your Back

We have been best friends since first grade—that's 38 years! We spent elementary, middle, and high school together, were roommates in college, and the maid of honor in each other's weddings. We were there for the birth of our children, the ups and downs of marriage, the ailments of parents, the unexpected disappointments. Being present is a big part of friendship, but it's not the most important thing. After all, there are other people who are present for all of these things—your family, your priest, your neighbor.

Rather, we think a deep friendship like ours has survived because we believe in each other—no matter what. It's the feeling that someone always has your back, would always pick you for her team, would drop everything to be by your side if needed. When I am down, she is my unflinching confidant, reminding me that this, too, will pass. When she has a huge success, I am her biggest cheerleader—reminding her that she has always been this wonderful, whether it was recognized before or not. When I am not living up to the kind of person she thinks I am, she is as steady as my conscience, nudging me in a small, sure voice to do what I know is right. There are no secrets, no judgments, no material expectations—we rarely give gifts to each other anymore because we both cherish and understand that. No gift can be more precious than the friendship that we share. —HEIDI K.

Faithful are the wounds of a friend;
but the kisses of an enemy are deceitful.

—PROVERBS 27:6

The best thing about friendship is that it is blind:
It doesn't matter if you are black, white, brown,
American, Cuban, French, or Mexican
(like me) . . . we are all the same.

—MISAEL A.

according to a UCLA study, oxytocin is released as part of the stress response in women. It buffers the fight or flight response and actually promotes tending to children and gathering with other women. When women engage in these activities, it counters stress and produces a calming effect. Scientists say this response does not occur in men.

Friends,
like wine,
are best old.

—JUAN C.

A happy retirement is not about money—it's about friends. Researchers have found that out of 100 people interviewed, 25 percent were more satisfied after retirement, while 34 percent were less satisfied. The happy retirees had a stronger social support network of friends who listened to their concerns, valued their friendship, and provided emotional support.

ILLUSTRATION CREDITS